Cruisin' the Amazing Amazon
A Jungle Journey to Discover Jesus

KJV Version
Very **e**xciting **B**ible **S**chool® Curriculum
© 2001 Cook Communications Ministries. All rights reserved.

By respecting the following guidelines, you help us keep these quality products affordable. Thank you, from Cook Communications Ministries. Permission is granted to the original purchaser to reproduce this book, either in whole or part, for use with this VBS program only. No materials in this book may be reproduced for any commercial purpose. Scripture quotations, unless otherwise noted, are from

THE HOLY BIBLE, KING JAMES VERSION (KJV),

Managing Editors:	Janet Lee, Karen Pickering, Doug Schmidt
Editors:	Susan Parsons, Scott Stewart
Senior Designer:	Mike Riester
Design Assistants:	Theresa Conditt, Rachel Simpson
Illustrators:	Aline Heiser, Terri Starrett
Elementary Program:	Susan Parsons
Preschool Program:	Anita Edlund
Photography:	Don Jones
Music:	John DiModica, Susan Parsons
Cruisin' the Amazon™ CD:	In Focus Music

ACCENT PUBLICATIONS
Solid Bible Foundation
Published by Accent Publications
4050 Lee Vance View • Colorado Springs, CO 80918-7100 • Colorado Springs, CO/Paris, Ontario

Printed in U.S.A.

ISBN: 0-7814-3635-4

TABLE OF CONTENTS

DIRECTOR'S GUIDE

Introduction to *Cruisin' the Amazing Amazon*™	D•1
Introduction to VeBS®	D•2
Custom VeBS® Options	D•3-8
NEW! Alternative Uses	D•9
VeBS® as Outreach	D•9
Online Resources	D•10
VeBS® for Youth and VeBS® for Adults	
Using This Guide	D•11
NEW! Electronic Clip Art	D•12
Planning Calendar	D•12-13
Overview Chart	D•14
Key Players	D•15
Budget	D•16
Supplies	D•17-22
Registration	D•23
Attendance	D•23
Schedule	D•24
NEW! Puppet Option	D•25
Creating Site Destinations	D•26
Opening & Closing Assemblies	D•26
Opening Skits	D•27-36
Closing Program	D•37
Closing Skits	D•38-43
Mission Project	D•44-45
Spiritual Gifts	D•46
Spiritual Gifts Chart	D•47
Volunteers	D•47
Personnel Chart	D•48
Training Your Staff	D•49
Team Building	D•50
Devotions	D•51-56
Appreciate Your Staff!	D•57
Promote	D•58
Involve the Kids	D•58
Involve the Church	D•59
Involve the Community	D•59-60
More Promotional Ideas	D•60
Publicity Skit	D•61-62
Follow-up on Kids	D•63
Follow-up on Leaders	D•63
Follow-up on Families	D•64
Follow-up on the Church	D•64

ELEMENTARY SITE GUIDES

Site 1: *Nighttime Expedition*	1•1-17
Site 2: *Jungle Trek*	2•1-18
Site 3: *Treetop Retreat*	3•1-15
Site 4: *Danger Bend*	4•1-15
Site 5: *Forever Falls*	5•1-17

PRESCHOOL GUIDE

Overview Chart	P•2
Introduction	P•2-4
Supplies	P•4-8
Nighttime Expedition: Jesus our Guide	P•9-19
Jungle Trek: Jesus our Provider	P•20-30
Treetop Retreat: Jesus our Shelter	P•31-40
Danger Bend: Jesus our Defender	P•41-51
Forever Falls: Jesus our Rescuer	P•52-61

REPRODUCIBLE RESOURCES

Budget Chart	R•2
Reimbursement Form	R•3
Registration Card	R•4
Attendance Chart	R•5
Certificate of Completion	R•6
Leader Hints	R•7-12
Age Characteristics Charts	R•13-16
Song Lyrics	R•17
Sheet Music	R•18-36
Coloring Poster	R•37
Postcard Invitation	R•38
E-mail Paragraph	R•39
Bulletin Inserts	R•40
Prayer & Volunteer Flyers	R•41
Press Release	R•42
Director's Evaluation	R•43-44
Family & Staff Evaluations	R•45
Craft Patterns	R•46-49
Zeez Puppet Pattern	R•50-51
Chibi Puppet Pattern	R•52-54
Tar-Tar Puppet Pattern	R•55-56
Jojo Puppet Pattern	R•57-59
Pinkie Puppet Pattern	R•60-63
Transparency Introduction	R•64-66
Nighttime Expedition Mural	R•67
Jungle Trek Mural	R•68
Treetop Retreat Mural	R•69
Danger Bend Mural	R•70
Forever Falls Mural	R•71
Preschool Mural	R•72
Preschool Animal Patterns	R•73
Nocturnal Animal Cutouts	R•74
Foliage Cutouts	R•75
Canopy Cutouts	R•76
Water Animal Cutouts	R•77
T-Shirt Art	R•78
Salvation Guide	R•79-80
Related Reading Materials	R•81-84

A Jungle Journey to Discover Jesus™

CRUISIN' THE AMAZING AMAZON™ KJV Version

DIRECTOR'S GUIDE

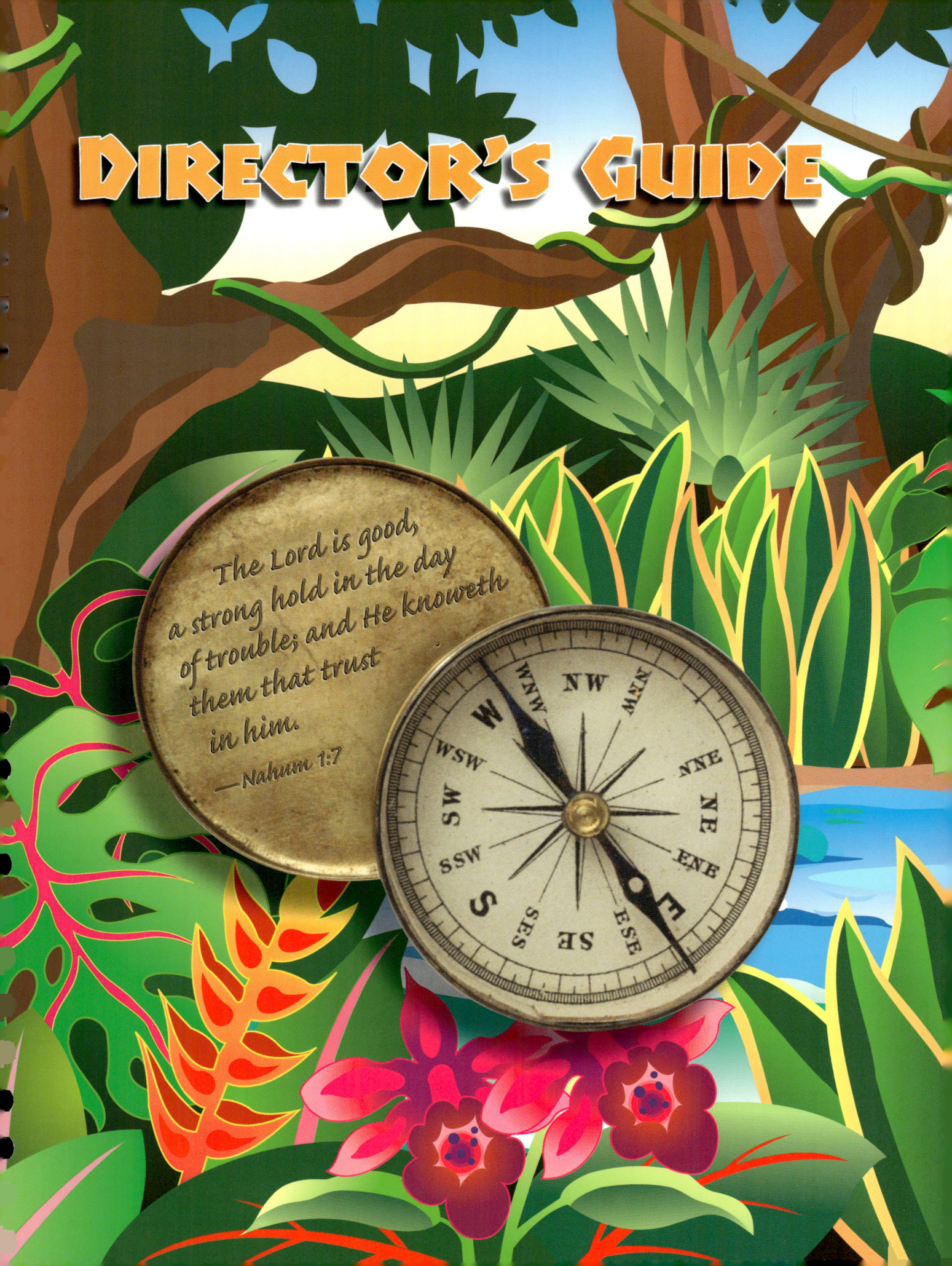

The Lord is good, a strong hold in the day of trouble; and He knoweth them that trust in him.
—Nahum 1:7

social media
DONE RIGHT

SOCIAL MEDIA DONE RIGHT

In this section we'll be covering Social Media Done Right in three easy steps:
1. *Know and Speak to Your Ideal Team Member or Client*
2. *Create Captivating Content Using the B.E.S. Strategy*
3. *Convert Your Followers to Consumers and Team Members*

Katy here! Before I discovered online marketing, I was a seventh grade Reading teacher. I spent years creating lesson plans that would connect students to the universal struggles of characters across a variety of genres. I knew that if my students felt connected to the characters, they were sold on the story. Connection, when it comes to any type of marketing, is the key to converting potential followers into lifelong believers.

> "Connection, when it comes to any type of marketing, is the key to converting potential followers into lifelong believers."

As Melanie and I started focusing on our VISION for the *Direct Sales Done Right Planner*, we had to take a walk down memory lane. I clearly remember seeing Melanie talk about the business opportunity and thinking, "That's so weird. I would never do that." Of course that was my initial thought, but a few months later I joined her. A huge part of why I joined Melanie's direct sales business as a distributor is because she painted a picture of possibility for me. When I first saw her talk about her business, I didn't see myself in that role! However, a few months of consistent content made me curious about what the opportunity could look like for me. Her approach to the business and her consistent messaging made me want to learn more. This approach Melanie was modeling is called:

The Network Marketer's Signature Style (def.)
The distributor's unique marketing spin on the product, service or the experience they offer that sets them apart from the other distributors in the company.

In other words, it's how you do things a little bit differently than others in the company. Creating the **Network Marketer's Signature Style** starts with understanding your intentional social media marketing strategy. In the quiz below, check off each box that you CONFIDENTLY believe describes your current social media.

Social Media Quiz

- [ ] I believe in the mission of my company.
- [ ] I believe in the products and services I offer.
- [ ] I believe that I can mentor others to succeed through the opportunity.
- [ ] I talk about the business opportunity consistently.
- [ ] I confidently share content that feels "unposed" and real.
- [ ] I authentically engage with my audience and it never feels "salesy."
- [ ] People often share my content because of the value I add.
- [ ] I don't scramble to post. I purposefully create content that is directly connected to my marketing plan.
- [ ] I create an opportunity for my followers to engage with my content but they are also engaging with one another.
- [ ] I see my platform as an online community where I serve my audience before I ever sell.
- [ ] I genuinely enjoy conversing with the people who show up on my social platforms.
- [ ] My audience relates to my content; it is relevant to them.
- [ ] I LISTEN to my audience and share content that they request.
- [ ] I showcase the wins of my team members.
- [ ] Followers naturally ask me about the products and services.
- [ ] I convert followers into clients through natural conversation and excitement for what I have to offer.
- [ ] I am growing a loyal community that creates a constant pipeline for invitations, follow ups, and testimonials.

TOTAL:

If you scored 1-5 that means there's a disconnect between you and your ideal client! Let's get to work!

If you scored 6-10 that means you are on your way to growing a strong, unique brand, but your messaging may need to be tweaked!

If you scored 11-17 that means that you have a solid brand and the goal is to continue creating content in a way that attracts your ideal client and team member.

So, how did you do? Let's be honest, NO ONE checks off all the boxes, and that's okay! The goal of your marketing is to focus on progress over perfection. Pay attention to what your audience LOVES and what you can do to create more engagement! Answering these questions is EXACTLY why we've created the **Network Marketer's Signature Style**. Direct sales is work, yes, but it's also meant to be fun.

Your social media doesn't need to be a source of stress. It's meant to generate more conversations, more opportunity, and more impact!

Happy clients are created when they feel they are being served before they've even signed up or made a purchase. Many times, those happy clients become our strongest team members. Finding space on the loud platforms we call social media is not hard to do, but online marketers RARELY take the time to do it. Are you ready to drown out the noise? Let's go!

> *"WARNING: Trust, connection, and community take time to foster and grow."*

Too often we want to rush the sale instead of slowing down enough to ASK what our followers REALLY want from us. What people really want has little to do with the actual products and much more to do with the feelings associated with them. Implementing these strategies takes time, consistency, and reflection. You won't see changes immediately, but imagine where you will be after 52 weeks of using the *Direct Sales Done Right Planner*! Imagine how good it's going to feel to know that you're generating leads by INTENTIONALLY just being you!

Problem, Desire, Solution

"But would you follow you?" This is one of my favorite questions to ask when I mentor women during the Chic Branding Experience Mentorship calls.

"Would you follow you?"

It's one of the most effective questions to ask because the answer almost always is, "I don't know," followed by something like:
"I just don't know what to say that hasn't been said."
"I feel like no one would really want to listen to me."
"I don't want to come off as too salesy."

Sound familiar?! And here's what I almost always respond with.

"Your brand isn't about you. It's about the problems you can resolve for the people around you."

When we write FOR our audience instead of TO our audience, there are three key questions to consider:
- *What problem are they experiencing that I can help resolve?*
- *What does my ideal client or team member really desire?*
- *What solution can I offer?*

We used to believe the most effective way to build a personal brand is to give people a look into your personal life, to pull back the curtain and let them in on WHO you are. But that brings up a pretty critical question: Why should they care?

When people are consuming our content, they likely watch it because it "serves them." They come back to our content because we "consistently serve them" and they likely purchase and sign up with us because they believe you can resolve a problem or support their desired lifestyle through the solution you are sharing (your products and your business opportunity).

When we take ourselves OUT of the picture, we free ourselves to serve others intentionally.

Review your content and ask yourself, "Do I make my ideal clients feel seen and heard?" When we make it less of a "personal brand" and more of an "INTENTIONAL brand", we become more ourselves with less worry, self-doubt, and fear!

Are you ready to dig into the 3 steps to Social Media Done Right?

1. Know and Speak to Your Ideal Team Member or Client

One of the biggest struggles women in direct sales have is creating authentic connections. Often we hear:
- "Who do I invite?"
- "How do I not come off as salesy?"
- "I feel like I am talking to myself!"
- "I am afraid to share the opportunity!"

Listen, it doesn't matter how many people you have following you. If you're not authentically connecting with your audience, your followers won't convert to customers.

Here's the secret: create content that feels inviting so that you never have to send "awkward" invites again! I see the word "invite" not just as one simple action but as the emotion we create on our feed. I want to make people "feel" invited, so I don't have to cross my fingers and hope that a stranger will say yes when I drop into their DMs with a message that starts with "Hey, girl!"

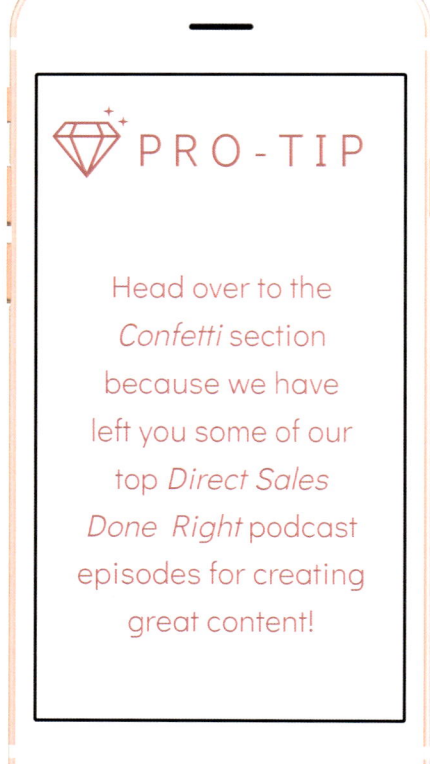

PRO-TIP

Head over to the Confetti section because we have left you some of our top Direct Sales Done Right podcast episodes for creating great content!

People crave connection, so the first question I encourage you to ask is, "Am I showing up for others or am I simply showing up to check off a box?" The second question is, "Am I showing up to sell a product or am I showing up to serve my audience?" Creating captions that include the audience shifts the focus from you (the writer) to them (the audience). For example, when you are sharing the products or the services you are selling, do you create a caption that gives the feeling of "look at me" or a feeling of "look at what can be"?

Does your content shout to the audience "So what?!" or does it sound like, "Ok, maybe I can do this, too." Inspire others to do what you do rather than just liking what you do. Focus on serving! What you share isn't about you, it's about what you can do for others.

2. Create Captivating Content Using the B.E.S. Strategy

I really tried to make the acronym work out for the B.E.S.T., but there didn't seem to be a need to add a letter and cause confusion. So, let's focus on the B.E.S. instead of B.E.S.T. Practices for Direct Sales Content Creation. Ask yourself, "Am I serving the top highlights of my life, or am I showing up to serve the person on the other side of the screen?" As a direct seller, we have to create content for our audience. People crave honesty, simplicity, and consistency. The good news is, we aren't creating Kardashian-style content where people feel like they need to keep up for the sake of—well, geez, does anyone know why they need to keep up with the Kardashians?! Instead, we are creating content for our audience—content that serves them, content that excites them, and content that is designed to help them take action. Here's what my clever little acronym actually stands for:

- Brand Awareness: You are making people aware of how you do business differently than others in your industry and other similar industries. It's more INTENTIONAL than PERSONAL.
- Engagement: You serve your audience with content that is entertaining, value-add, and usually somewhat binge-worthy so it elicits engagement.
- Sales: This is the content that educates your audience on the current problem they may be experiencing and the desire they have, and ultimately provides a solution you can offer!

> *I want to let you in on a little secret. If you want to be seen, get out of traffic! Stop trying to please the masses, and make your message meaningful to the people that you truly want to connect with.*

PRO-TIP

SCAN the QR CODE to hear Katy talk in-depth about the B.E.S. Strategy

BRAND AWARENESS

You will begin positioning yourself as an expert vs. a personal brand owner. Ultimately brand awareness lets people see your unique approach to your work. This gives your audience a glimpse of how you serve, what you care about, and why you may be a good guide. We don't focus on "sales" as much as "expertise" through this type of content. It gives people a feel for what it would be like to be served by you.

ENGAGEMENT

Through this type of content, we want to ensure that your audience is taking action and engaging with your content so that they continue to come back because they feel connected to you. Engagement content supports growth/reach, media goals, and builds trust with your audience.

SALES

How is working with you different from other people in the industry? What experience do you offer through your community for your clients? Add evidence of your SATISFIED customers and team members!

Of course we want our content to feel inviting, but you are likely wondering, "How!?" Here's the deal, we want our ideal team member or client to *do something* or *think something* immediately with our content. In order to do that, we need to create calls to action *(CTA)* or calls to think *(CTT)* while using the B.E.S. Strategy.

Let's be real, as marketers, social media can feel like you're stuck in a traffic jam on I-95, looking for the nearest exit! Even if the back roads take a little longer, you can rest assured that it's better than staying stuck. Am I right?! I mean, standing out means that we sometimes have to slow down, pay attention to the signs and occasionally reroute!

If you want to make a massive impact with your business, great! Great! But first, we must focus on serving small! Here are a few of my go-to, tried and true tips:

Stop the Scroll

First, to stop the scroll, you need a captivating image with a matching tagline (the first sentence of your text or the written content in your reel). I love sharing a relatable story starter with just enough details to connect from the start! If my audience can visualize themselves in my story, I know they will pause to read more! *For example, "I stood in the bathroom mirror, pinching my love handles with tears in my eyes, and all I could think to myself was ... how did you let yourself go?"*

Create a Pause

The pause is where the magic happens because it's the bridge between engagement and scroll on. The pause creates the connection, and connection builds trust. The pause is where they decide to click "see more" and read the entire caption, or they scroll on.
If someone is showing up for you, you must let them know that you are listening. Engagement forces us to slow down, to think about our words, and to interact with those who are processing our content. In the example above where I talked about the love handles, I go on to describe how the reader might be feeling so that I could connect with their problem.

Get to the Point

I keep my sentences short using italics, ellipses, or even emojis to keep my followers reading. I pay attention to small details that connect me to them, whether that's the music I listen to, the way I mother my kids, or some of my childhood pop culture memories.

You want to show people that when they comment you are going to be there to respond. This creates a personal connection between you and the individual follower (remember we are speaking to individuals, not masses). It is the foundation of how relationships are built.

When you cultivate conversation, think about it as a drip of dopamine: you want to come back for more. This reinforces the followers' commenting behavior and increases the likelihood that they will interact the next time you post. It's not just a post anymore; it's an opportunity to cultivate community.

Stick Around

When I post I make sure to stick around for a little while and engage with people as they're commenting. This will boost your engagement on the post and the platform will recognize this content as "valuable" and show it to more people.

Then, take the next steps. If someone likes, comments, or watches, this is what I call "eye contact". If someone is kind enough to check you out, reciprocate! Engage with their account. Take note of their life and look for opportunities to connect on their page.

If You Sound Like a Broken Record, You're Doing It Right

It's okay if your content bores you. Shocking, I know! But it should bore you. Why? Because it's not about you! Your content is about serving others. So you'll sometimes feel like you're repeating yourself. That's a good thing! But for now, remember that your audience is always leaving you clues about what they enjoy, what they want to see more of, and what doesn't connect. Listen to your audience!

Bottom line, conversation—authentic, light and meaningful conversation—is what makes conversion possible.

3. Convert Your Followers to Consumers and Team Members

Conversion is simplified when you have common ground. It will never feel icky when you FEEL as though you've been serving people long before you've made an offer. I find that my audience gets excited to hear about products, experiences, services, or joining my team after they've been engaging with me, getting to know me, and cultivating a social connection!

It's kind of like dating, isn't it? Over time, trust is built around common connections. TRUTHBOMB: TRUST TAKES TIME! If you're focused on selling instead of serving, you won't convert followers into clients. Especially in direct sales, it's our responsibility to make sure we are sharing our products and services in a way that feels authentic. You build trust over time with each post that you create. **Every story you tell bridges the gap between who you are and how you can serve your audience.** Remember, a successful post isn't determined by a set number of likes or comments, it's when the post creates meaningful conversation. For more information on how to create trust visit: *chicinfluencer.com/free-resources*

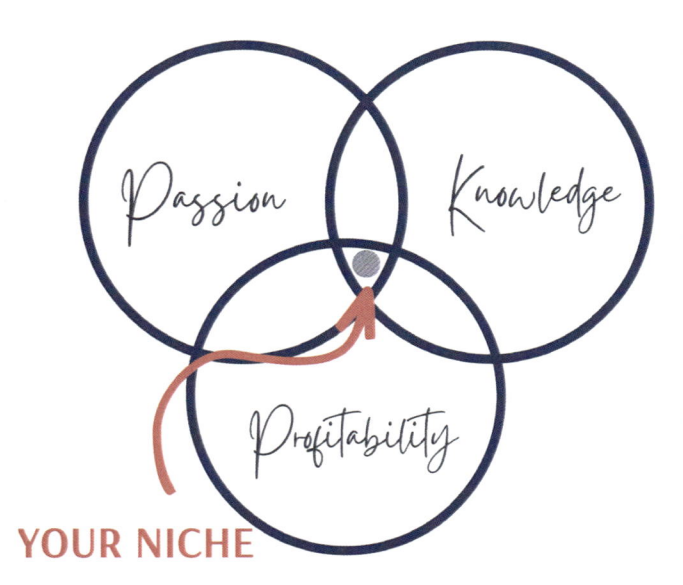

FINDING YOUR NICHE

I really think of this as the icing on the cake. Your niche is what makes you unique as a human and creates the trust factor we talked about in the Network Marketer's Signature Style.

There are three areas to consider when creating your niche:
1. Passion
2. Knowledge
3. Profit

In order to avoid confusing your audience, select ONE key topic (niche) you want to talk about consistently on your platform. There are so many people marketing on social media, so to establish yourself as a PROFESSIONAL business owner, we encourage you to clarify what ONE idea you want to serve and repeat often. Here is how we at Chic suggest you identify your niche.

When you have a clear understanding of your knowledge, your passion, and how you profit (through the products as well as the opportunity), you begin to clarify your specific niche. No one can do business quite like you, and no one can provide the same experience to the direct sales business that you can. With a clear understanding of your niche, your content should speak to your ideal customer/team member's current struggles and desires and provide them with a plausible solution. The key is creating content that serves well.

I don't know how many customer avatar trainings I've listened to over the course of eleven years, but really, finding your niche is simple. The key is to not overthink it.

Passion + Knowledge + Profit = Niche. That's it. That's the message.

Identify your passion. Connect it to your knowledge. Bring it back to how you serve through your products and your opportunity, and you have found your niche. No avatar training is required.

In 2012, one of the first marketing posts that I wrote had an image of my products and the cryptic words, "Decide. Commit. Succeed," followed by a hyperlink to purchase a starter kit. Needless to say, no one purchased my product on that day, and for the weeks that followed, it seemed that I was just not cut out for this whole network marketing thing. It took me an absurd amount of time to realize that people didn't want a link (not yet anyway). I needed time to establish my credibility by serving my audience well. Posting a link with a few words and crossing my fingers that someone would sign up wasn't a successful business strategy. As I started to get curious about what drove people to ask questions, what made people comment on my posts, and how I could be different in the industry, I realized it all had a lot to do with niche (passion, knowledge, and profit). What drew people to learn more was the unique way that I served them. Interestingly enough, the more I served, the more I sold.

For example, when I (Katy) decided to niche down and share more boldly, I began sharing tips to help content writers perfect their unique style. It gave me an opportunity to share my passion for writing, my knowledge on the subject, and became a natural opportunity to share what I offer as a service.

Likewise, I (Melanie) used to talk about wellness, fashion, my family, and business. I have shifted my focus to solely talking about direct sales team building and leadership. I love sharing advice for network marketers on how to navigate through the different seasons of business growth, how to build strong and healthy downlines, and what systems you need in place so that you can scale without burning out. You will notice that my social media very specifically speaks to women in direct sales. I share the rest of my life in my stories, but my feed is for my niche!

Your Unique Spin on the Business

People are curious about why you do what you do. It's true! People may not understand the business model or why you love your company. They may cast judgment or tell you the model doesn't work. But mark my words, they are curious.

They are curious about WHY and HOW you run your business. I (Katy) remember watching Melanie talk about her business thinking, "That is so weird! Who works out for fun? Who attends live workout 'events' that aren't classes? I didn't understand it, but I was curious. Showcasing the opportunity isn't about highlighting your achievements, it's about highlighting the possibility for others.

People are more likely to join your team if they believe that you can guide them to succeed!

Showcasing yourself as a business mentor and embedding your values into your content is a great way to connect with your potential clients or prospects! Showing the impact the business has had on your own life as well as your team members provides social evidence and boosts your confidence. It is not bragging.

In fact, if your life has been impacted by the opportunity, it's selfish not to share.

Your confidence in the business opportunity will grow the more you share the business with people. Through sharing our small wins along the way and inviting people to join our teams, we created top organizations in the company. Small wins matter!!!

HOW DO I TALK ABOUT THE BUSINESS?
Melanie and I (Katy) believe there are 5 areas of impact when running a business. These impact factors allow you to share the wins with your audience that they can relate to.

1. Financial Impact

People relate to wins like getting the groceries paid or being able to pay for your kid's hockey gear. It isn't about how BIG the wins are. It's about how relatable they are!

2. Physical Impact

This is especially true for those in the wellness industry. Have you made morning routines part of your life? How does that impact how you show up? Did your new nutritional or fitness plan transform your life or the lives of your clients/team members? Share it!

3. Emotional Impact

Do you find joy through your work? Purpose? How have you been transformed from the inside out?

4. Social Impact

Do you do business with a community of like-minded women? What does that look like? How do you live out "collaboration over competition" daily?

5. Spiritual Impact

Has your business deepened your spiritual beliefs? How? Share!

Although every area may not relate to your own life, I would venture that at least 3-4 of them do! If you are new to the business, lean on the impact that others have experienced! Don't worry about how far along you are. Focus on sharing the vision of where you are going!

Need support achieving your recruitment goals? Consider The Rockstar Recruitment Course with Melanie Mitro!

2 vision casting DONE RIGHT

VISION CASTING DONE RIGHT

I (Katy) was first introduced to the concept of "visualizing" on a business training call by a leader in our direct sales industry. I was only about two weeks into owning my own business, and I was already overwhelmed. I remember her sharing this incredible story of how she pictured her wedding overlooking the Amalfi Coast at sunset. She walked through every breathtaking detail of the majestic day, and at the end of the call, she shared her wedding pictures that showed she had indeed made her vision a reality.

I was completely spellbound, up until moments after the call. I had a sink filled with dishes and spit up running down my shoulder. When I thought about creating a vision, I couldn't think of anything more out-of-reach. Her vision was inspiring of course, but as a woman who had never "visualized" and whose reality was a full-time job, dirty dishes, and an argument over finances just waiting to happen, it actually didn't move me to action. It paralyzed me.

Since that time, I've heard countless speakers talk about vision and manifestation. Most of them share the concept the same way: "Dream big," and, "Take massive action!" And while I can appreciate their excitement about the BIG vision, I think we often forget a critical step.

Here's the deal. Vision boards are pretty. I mean, who doesn't want to create a 7-figure business, or develop 6-pack abs, or build a dream home with a dream

30

car in the garage and a white picket fence in the front yard?

I get it. You have to picture what you want, draw a line in the sand, and— BOOM—take massive action. Visualize it. Build it. And straight up "FIELD OF DREAMS" style, it will come.

Until it doesn't come.

Until that vision board you took such care to create ends up buried under a pile of unread personal development books.

Until that picture you wanted gets blurred out by rejection, by "I can't," and by the reality of daily responsibility.

Until that vision board gets put away for another day, another month, another year, another life. Sound familiar? Here's what can make the difference between the vision of what you want and the reality of what you are working toward:

You cannot sit idly by waiting for the vision to be manifested. You have to care more about the action than the outcome. You have to take really boring, mundane, and sometimes SLOW, seemingly insignificant action every day. Sure, your vision board matters if, AND ONLY if, you are taking the RIGHT action DAILY that will help you achieve it.

And let's be real, that part isn't pretty. No one throws a "get gritty party" (but maybe I should, I don't know. I'd totally bring cake). No one wants to glorify the grit.

I see it all the time: Push goals, vision parties, and manifestation meetings. Medidate. Visualize. Pump your arms. Dream BIG.

"IT WILL HAPPEN!" It won't.

For visualization to work, you have to believe that you are CAPABLE of making that vision a reality. If it feels out of reach, it will be out of reach. If your GRAND VISION doesn't feel attainable, we need to shift our focus to mile markers along the way to achieving that GRAND VISION. I call this concept "Driving Toward Daylight". In other words, we have to blur out the end destination and allow our eyes to focus on the smaller achievements (mile markers) that are attainable because they are right in front of us.

Driving Toward Daylight

Let's break down how to cast a vision we can actually achieve.

1. Cast the Big Vision

Make it clear and feel it with all of your senses so that the thought of not achieving it actually aches—straight up hurts. For example, when I visualized the home we bought five years ago, I didn't just picture the big windows or the hardwood floors. I pictured the muddy shoes and popsicles in the freezer. I pictured the sounds of a crackling fire and the scent of homemade pumpkin bread on a Saturday afternoon. The picture was so clear in my mind that the thought of something taking it away actually pained me.

2. Blur Out the Big Vision

This is critical. Take your hand and blur out that big vision! I know, I know. Sounds strange, but blur that baby out. Our attention and focus doesn't need to be on the end result. It needs to be on the action. Yes, our vision is still there; we are driving toward THIS, our daylight. But our eyes need to be on the smaller vision right in front of us!

3. Focus On Your Mile Markers

Align your vision to action. In the next section, Melanie will walk you through how to set smaller, attainable goals in your business throughout the year that drive you toward your vision. Remember, setting smaller, achievable goals keeps your eyes focused on the action that leads to the desired outcome. These are the action steps that NEED to be taken daily. These mile markers tell you how much you have left to go as you close the gap between where you are NOW and where you want to be (daylight). In our planner, we have an entire section dedicated to your mile markers called the *Income Producing Activity Tracker*, which can be found on page 56.

4. Divorce Yourself from the Idea of Perfect Action

Imperfect action is much better than perfect inaction. Life happens! If it doesn't go as planned, revisit your mile markers.

5. Celebrate the Small Wins Along the Way!

As we set smaller goals and begin to see results, we gain confidence and continue moving forward to the next mile marker and the next and the next (you get the picture)!

A personal note from Katy about casting the BIG VISION:

Although I found other people's big visions inspiring, I knew that I needed to create my own VISION. <u>For me, the BIG vision I set to achieve through direct sales was paying for the groceries.</u> That, to me, was a BIG DEAL. It meant no more fighting over enough in the account. It meant I didn't have to feel guilty about purchasing diapers before payday. It felt attainable to me AND it excited me. As this became consistently achievable, I cast another vision of extending my maternity leave. Then I cast another and another.

My point is this: Never let anyone tell you that your vision isn't grand enough. If it excites you and motivates you, that's what counts. After all, it's YOUR daylight that you are driving toward.

Never let anyone tell you your vision isn't grand enough.

Scan the QR Code to watch Katy's video on Driving Toward Daylight!

next UP...

3
goal setting
DONE RIGHT

GOAL SETTING DONE RIGHT

Setting clear and defined goals is ESSENTIAL when it comes to creating a solid strategy for your social media. Every single successful business owner has the ability to connect their income and growth goals to their marketing strategy.

I (Melanie) sometimes feel like we spend a lot of time setting our business goals and then we set separate social media goals. The problem is that your social media goals are not supporting your business goals, but they should. Your social media goals and content should be directly related to your bottom line. After all, the reason you are creating social media content is to grow your know, like, and trust factor so that you can create more sales, right?

In this section, we are going to ensure that our social media content is directly correlated to our business goals. There will be no more throwing spaghetti at the wall to see what sticks. Our social media has a purpose. Whether it's to connect or call your followers to action, there is always a point to what we are putting out there. So let's dig into goal setting.

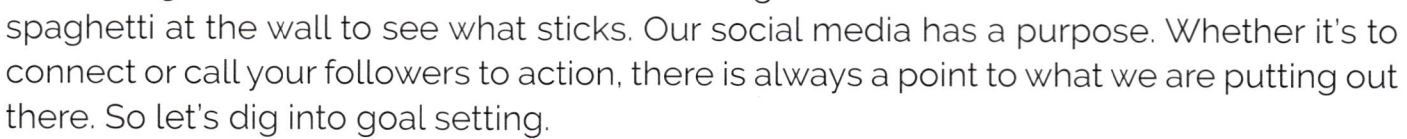

There are two parts to goal setting. You have annual goals and then you have smaller goals built upon each other to achieve the end goal. The mile markers consist of quarterly, monthly, weekly, and daily benchmarks that add up to reaching the annual goals. One of our gifts is being able to see the big picture of the end goal and break it down into smaller, more manageable quarterly, monthly, weekly, and daily activities. I believe that in order to effectively communicate your message you have to be clear on the objective and the end goal you are working towards.

Chic Your YEAR
Start with the big picture of what you want to achieve before jumping into creating con-

tent. First, ask yourself, what are your two to three main goals for the next twelve months? Where do you want to be a year from now? What kind of direct sales business do you want to have? What is your unique approach to your company's products? How many customers do you want to serve in the next year? How much income are you earning? How many subscribers do you have on your email list? How many people are a part of your community? How big is your team? Go ahead and brain dump all of your thoughts onto a sheet of paper.

This is where you have to allow yourself to dream big and get a little uncomfortable with what you want your business to look like one year from today. How do you want your social media to support your business goals?

Don't get stuck in knowing EXACTLY where you want to be at the end of the year. When I create yearly goals, it can sometimes be a leap of faith and sometimes a stab in the dark. I am not sure exactly what will happen over the next twelve months. What I do is review the previous year and estimate potential growth. I set an income goal that is over and above the year before. I always aim to grow by at least 25% or more. I set an income goal that challenges me but isn't so completely unrealistic that it causes me to freeze.

There is nothing wrong with tweaking your goals during the year if things aren't going as planned. Not setting goals because we are afraid we won't reach them is where the problem lies. So, don't overthink this section. Let's set some goals!

Below, I've given you a few examples. Please note how each goal is S.M.A.R.T. Writing a S.M.A.R.T goal means that it is *Specific, Measurable, Attainable, Realistic* and *Timely*.
EXAMPLES MIGHT INCLUDE:

12 Month Goals:

1. I will make $10,000 in my direct sales business by December 31st, 2024.

2. I will advance my business to the Director rank by July 2024.

3. I will earn the company's rewards trip in August 2024.

Now it's your turn! Remember to make your goals specific, measurable, and realistic, yet challenging and timely! You don't have to have three goals, but make sure the goals you set feel like they will help you grow in the direction you envision your business going.

My 12 Month Goals:

1.

2.

3.

The next step is to divide each goal into four quarters.

NOTE, it does not matter if you start this planner in July or in January. The goal is to start NOW and not wait until a fresh week, month, or year.

In the next four months, what will you accomplish? This requires baseline data. Take a look at your current business and ask yourself where you are today and what is realistic for you to accomplish in the next four months.

For example, you decide you want to earn $10,000 in commissions with your direct sales business by December 31, 2024.

Let's break it down: I want to earn $10,000. If I divide that over the four quarters of the year, that means I am earning $2,500 per quarter, and thus $833.33 a month.

Does that feel doable? If so, then you have set a goal that is doable yet challenging.

By setting this monthly goal you can now create a list of ways to always be focused on increasing your sales. For example, if my main focus is sales, I might focus on upselling customers with my favorite products when creating a shopping cart for them. I can run a VIP group where I do product demonstrations, use social media to address my ideal target clients' problems, and do online parties where my focus is customer sales.

Once you have clarity on your goals, you should always be aligning your daily to-do list to your goals.

We will be going over how to create more strategies to reach your goals in the next section too.

Let's Take Action!

So now it's your turn. Write out your goals for the next twelve months, break them down, and then chart out your quarterly game plan.

EXAMPLES MIGHT INCLUDE:
YEARLY GOALS:
Goal 1: I will make $10k in my direct sales business by December 31, 2024.
Baseline: In 2023, I made $6K in commissions from my direct sales business.

Goal 2. I will advance my business to the rank of Director by July 2024.
Baseline: What is your current rank_____.

Goal 3. I will earn the company's rewards trip in August 2024.
Baseline: I have earned X amount of trip points so far towards the trip.

QUARTER 1	QUARTER 2	QUARTER 3	QUARTER 4
Goal 1 Generate $2,500 in income through my direct sales business	Goal 1 Generate $2,500 in income through my direct sales business	Goal 1 Generate $2,500 in income through my direct sales business	Goal 1 Generate $2,500 in income through my direct sales business
Goal 2 Enroll 6 consultants to my team	Goal 2 Advance to Director	Goal 2 Enroll 5 consultants to my team	Goal 2 Advance to Executive Director
Goal 3 Earn 1/4 of trip points	Goal 3 Earn 1/4 of trip points	Goal 3 Earn 1/4 of trip points	Goal 3 Earn 1/4 of trip points

QUARTER 1	QUARTER 2	QUARTER 3	QUARTER 4
Goal 1	Goal 1	Goal 1	Goal 1
Goal 2	Goal 2	Goal 2	Goal 2
Goal 3	Goal 3	Goal 3	Goal 3

Creating Your Roadmap

Now that we've set those goals, it's time to create a roadmap to achieve those goals. Your content drives you closer to your year end goals. Every week in your planner you are going to track your progress towards your goal, what your wins were, what your challenges were, and how you will address them in the next week.

We are going to walk you through a month of planning for your direct sales business (see page 44-45 for an example calendar).

Every month we ask ourselves a series of questions:
- What is my personal sales goal?
- What is my personal recruitment goal?
- What are some of the known obstacles we will face (vacations, holidays, back to school, trends of consumers based on market research)?
- Do I have any sales/project deadlines this month?
- Are there any new product launches, sales, or promotions I want to run?
- How will I get ahead of and plan for these challenges so my business maintains steady growth?

Example: We've come to realize that, historically, social media in December is quieter for our audience. Many of them are prepping for the holidays and gearing up for the kids' winter break. Most working mommas are running around like chickens with their heads cut off taking care of Christmas shopping, party plans, end-of-year launches or sales, and maintaining regular house tasks.

We also know that during December women are a little more strapped for cash (known obstacle) and are less likely to invest in a product that is going to require sacrifice or a new routine. We have to consider that in our marketing plan.

Understanding this trend means we are going to focus on handling objections, offering advice on how to plan for the craziness of December, and tailor our services in a way that meets the needs of the very busy and cash-strapped woman. Make sense?

> **PRO-TIP**
>
> Write the launch date for whatever product or service you are promoting. What is the last possible day people can purchase? Then, you work backwards. Count 10-14 days before the goal date. That is the FIRST day you will begin marketing your promotion.

We know that being intentional starts with a heavier emphasis on marketing in the first part of the month. This way we're not scrambling close to the holidays to close sales or feeling like we're pushing people towards our own agenda. The rest of the month we consistently serve our audience, speak to their biggest struggles, and show them possible solutions through our offerings.

Next, we pull out the blank monthly calendar and we start writing our marketing game plan.

The reason we take 10-14 days to promote a product is because our audience needs to hear the message multiple times before they commit. Remember, it's normal for a very small number of your followers to see your content, so the more you relay a message, the higher the likelihood that your followers will convert to clients.

Now we create ideas for marketing our promotion. We start by asking ourselves:
- What about that product is unique or different?
- Who is this product/service for?
- Why should people buy it from you and not someone else?
- Why are you the best person for the job?
- What is your unique angle and spin on what you do?
- What do people ask you for advice about over and over?
- What questions will people have about what you are offering?
- What are the different post ideas that you can write that will help you promote this product/service/experience?
- What format are you going to create this content in? Reels? Stories? IG Live?
- What are the stories you can create that support the marketing message each day?

We want to begin thinking about our ideal client's problems, their desires as well as their potential objections, their possible questions, and most importantly, our unique spin!

The more clearly we can answer these questions, the more likely that our audience will connect with us.

This is your brainstorming session. Get all of your ideas out on paper so you can begin to make sense of it all. As you look at this sheet of paper, start to organize everything into your weekly plan. Take the big, messy ideas you've brainstormed and create a weekly marketing layout.

PRO-TIP

Keep your marketing focus on ONE major marketing theme weekly. It's important to remember that your audience won't likely see ALL of your content, so you don't want to confuse them with multiple messages. Occasionally, it's okay to market something small, like a pop-up sale or launch that you know will quickly sell out.

month
January

- [x] Complete End-Of-Month Reflection (see previous page)
- [x] Review My Vision
- [x] Update Monthly Goals
- [x] Set My Marketing Focus
- [x] Create Monthly Marketing Calendar
- [x] Communicate with those Involved

monthly goals
- 100 people in free group
- sell 20 winter skin care kits
- $833.33 in sales
- sign 2 new team members
- goal: 20 people interested in webinar

marketing focus
- new product launch
- FREE GROUP: how to winter proof your skin
- BIZ OPP make beauty your biz

SAMPLE MARKETING CALENDAR

MONDAY	TUESDAY	WEDNESDAY
1	2 announce free group, start adding	3
8	9	10
5 day free group: winter proof your skin		
15 *customer sales goal met!	16	17 *start inviting to webinar
22	23	24 biz opp event: make beauty your biz event!
29	30	31 last day to sign new consultants!

44

"Every, and I do mean every, marketing plan must lead with the 'give', not with the 'buy'" - Katy

THURSDAY	FRIDAY	SATURDAY	SUNDAY
4	5	6	7
11	12	13	14
18	19	20	21
	pre-webinar inviting and marketing		
25	26	27	28
post event invites, follow ups, and social			

next UP...

planning
DONE RIGHT

4

PLANNING DONE RIGHT

Now that we have BIG goals set, we have the BIG vision of where we want to go, and now we're really ready to start doing the work! Full disclosure, numbers and stats have never been my (Katy's) jam. In fact, part of me still twitches when I think of Mike (my husband) and his weekly Excel budget sheets. But when it comes to understanding the trends in my business, numbers and stats are like unlocking the great algorithm mystery.

CONNECTION drives all content choices. I use my stats to help me decide how to serve my audience. Without my stats, I don't have a full picture of what's most effective. At best, I have a hunch. Using these stats allows me to create similar content, overcome potential objections, provide more context to a previous piece of content, and continue to serve well!

This section of the tracker has 4 main categories:
- Reflect & Refine
- My Income Producing Activity Tracker
- Weekly Social Media Plan
- End of Month Reflection

Reflect & Refine

In order to get where you want to go, you have to embrace and learn from where you've been. In this section, you will complete a weekly inventory of your wins. You'll have a clear picture of the content that did well through saves, shares, and engagement. This gives you an opportunity to grow and become more effective at serving your audience! By tracking your social media results, you can make intentional content decisions that impact the bottom line.

Please Note: In order to view your insights, you must have a Business or Creator account on Instagram and you must have a Business account on Facebook.

Tracking Your Social Media Stats

Analyzing our weekly social media trends is an important part of our growth because it gives us indisputable evidence about what our audience and new followers want to see, how well we are serving, and if our content is leading to conversion. As Melanie says, when we are intentional about our content, we don't just throw spaghetti at the wall, hoping something will stick. We know what our audience wants and we use that feedback to help us create the next week's social media marketing plan.

I will say it again, "Tracking reveals trends, trends reveal the truth, and the truth creates change!" Can I get an amen? Goodbye, guesswork; hello, strategic social media growth!

Tracking Results

Before setting new goals, we want to reflect on our habits from the previous week. We want to focus on the outcome and our output (our efforts). Both Melanie and I feel it takes a consistent 7-10 days to effectively market an idea, product, service, or experience for people to notice. And if we aren't seeing an impact on the bottom line, we might need to adjust our marketing.

Five areas are noted for tracking results:
- How many invitations did I send?
- How many customers did I enroll?
- How many team members did I enroll?
- How much income did I earn?
- How many new emails did I collect?

It's worth noting that INVITATIONS happen through conversation. When you are tracking your invitations, do not put an emphasis on the number of posts you do that call people to respond, but the actual conversations you have with an individual where you are inviting them to try your product, service, or experience.

Focus on tracking income or commissions you produce through the use of your social media. When it comes to enrollments, this should be specific to your current marketing efforts, whether you are focusing on enrollment into your VIP Launch Page, your team, your bootcamp, your email list, your new course, or even a product test group. (Enrollment is a specific number of people who've opted in because of your efforts!)

Tracking Your Wins for the Week

While analyzing the growth of your social media page it's important to take time and celebrate the wins of the week as well as acknowledge anything that you may want to adjust in the future. Being aware of how your audience is responding allows you to continue creating quality content that encourages engagement and ultimately leads to clients!

Business Goals for the Week

Let's get clear on our goals for the week ahead. Establish the specifics of your marketing efforts. What are you marketing? Are you focused on recruiting members to your team? Are you focused on your company's products? What is your personal goal with the marketing efforts? How are you going to market?

Once you've established your marketing goals for the week, you can begin creating quality content that will lead to conversion!

Examples:
- Enroll 2 new customers with the beauty bundle.
- Reach $500 in customer sales through one virtual party.

The next step is to make sure that I am creating my content for the week and it supports my goals. Remember, we highly recommend focusing on only one goal a week to avoid confusing your audience. See an example on the next page!

REFLECT & REFINE SAMPLE

January 21, 2024
WEEK ENDING

facebook

CURRENT NO. OF FOLLOWERS: 518
MOST ENGAGING POST: get ready with me routine
POST REACH: 1,062
POST ENGAGMENT: 380

instagram

ACCOUNTS REACHED: 6,217
NEW FOLLOWERS: 19
CURRENT FOLLOWERS: 3,532
MOST SAVED CONTENT: New Year's Resolutions (15)
MOST SHARED CONTENT: Funny skincare memes (22)
HIGHEST STORY VIEWS: 108
HIGHEST CONTENT REACH: 1,532 - 6 skincare truths
SHARES: 12 SAVES: 15 COMMENTS: 7

tiktok

VIDEO VIEWS: 1,724
PROFILE VIEWS: 50
FOLLOWERS: 2,003
TRENDING VIDEOS: weekly skincare routine

BUSINESS RESULTS

NO. OF INVITES SENT? 32
NO. OF TEAM MEMBERS ENROLLED? 1
NO. OF CUSTOMERS ENROLLED? 3
INCOME I EARNED? $200
NO. OF EMAILS COLLECTED: 10

👍 WINS FROM LAST WEEK

- the video/reel of my cosmetics shopping resonated with my audience

- my introvert content does well

🎯 BUSINESS GOALS FOR THE UPCOMING WEEK

- sign up 1 new rep on my team
- invite 50 people to the behind the makeup mask online event
- create $400 in online sales next week

📝 NOTES

- use the shopping concept to create a business post for next week

My Income Producing Activity (IPA) Tracker

The My Income Producing Activity Tracker (IPA) section is essential to driving the results in your business. We have learned over the years that anyone can make themselves "busy" doing work, but not everyone is busy doing the RIGHT work. The IPA tracker outlines the activities that you should be completing on a regular basis in order to get the results that you want. I know that tracking isn't necessarily the most glamorous and #intsaworthy part of direct sales, but it is the ONLY way you will see success. If you don't know your trends, you won't know the truth embedded in your daily actions. It's one thing to create content, but your content has to back up and support the private conversations you have with people. You NEED both conversations and social media content for success.

Let's break down the IPA tracker. The tasks listed are divided into three sections: *Community, Conversion,* and *Customer Service.* When these tasks are done consistently over time without the loss of enthusiasm, results compound.

Community
Community is where you are connecting and conversing with your ideal target audience (usually before any sale has occurred).

Adding followers can look like this: I go to my Facebook page where I search my kids' school district for a "parents of X district" closed Facebook group. I interact with parents in the group about common interests and send them a friend request. On Instagram, I might search #marsyouthbasketball and interact with other parents of players in our district. When I interact, that might look like watching their stories and sending a direct message related to what they shared, commenting on a relevant post, and following the account. Growing my community is essential to building a healthy pipeline of future customers.

Intentional connection is the next step. This is the part of the process where the person I engaged with in the first step responds and we are now in conversation. This is unrelated to my business. We are in the initial stages of developing a relationship. Think of this like going on a date. You are determining if you have the same core values and interests. You are not concerned about rushing to the invite process.

Creating your social media content is next. Make sure that is it related to your niche and use the B.E.S. Strategy to ensure you are aligned to your marketing goals.

We get asked all the time about how many pieces of content we should be sharing every day. Here is our rule of thumb. Ask yourself, "What does consistency look like for me?" Ask yourself, "How many times a day do I want to commit to showing up?" Then, commit to that. For example, if you know that posting one time a day is what you can commit to, then DO IT, but do it consistently because IT MATTERS!!!

7-10 stories is the task of uploading stories to your Facebook and/or Instagram daily. Your stories are a peek behind the curtain of who you are. Your stories should be your daily call to action in your business, plus content that connects people to who you are and what you like and stand for. This is a great way to just share daily life, ask your audience for their feedback, and have fun conversations.

Highlight my customers, team members or other social media accounts.
In this task you are focused on sharing social proof that what you provide works. Share testimonials, tag your current customers and product users, and share relevant content that relates to your personality and style. Personally, I (Melanie) do this in my stories. Social proof is one of the best ways to build the "know, like, and trust" factor. This section allows you to move from, "look at what I'm doing," to, "YOU CAN DO IT TOO!"

Conversion
The second section of the IPA tracker is conversion. In this section, we are focused on transitioning those initial conversations into invitations to the products and/or services that we have to offer.

DM (direct message) people who viewed, liked, commented on my stories and posts plus new followers. This task is where you are paying attention to who is engaging with your content and reaching out to start conversations. This is specific to what you sell or the services you offer.

PRO-TIP

We follow the 10% rule. Out of all the people you invite, 10% will say yes. Knowing the 10% rule allows you to back into the number of direct invites you need to send to reach your goal. For example, if I want to sign up 10 new community members this week, I need to send out 100 invites. I can split those invites up in any way that I would like.

For example, Sally voted on my poll about the free, healthy, glowing skin downloadable I created. Then I messaged Sally and said, "Hey Sally, I saw you voted on my poll about the downloadable. What is your email? I will send that right over to you!!!"

Direct invite to service, experience or product. This task means that you are going to be inviting people through private message to join you. Here is an example: "Hi Jenn, thanks so much for the love on my post about my fitness community. I currently have a spot in the community available if you would like the details. Let me know and I can get that right over to you."

Follow-ups. This task is simple and straightforward. You are following up with all the people you have invited to your product, service, or experience. We recommend waiting 24 hours before sending the first follow up. Then, we follow up until registration closes, the product is sold out, or the person doesn't want to be on our list anymore.

Ask for referrals. In this task you are going to your current customers and letting them know that you have another opportunity open for them to share with their friends and family. Asking for a referral can be done through a post in your VIP group, an email, a direct message, or text.

Customer Service

The last section of the IPA Tracker is customer service. In this section, you are nurturing and supporting your current clients so that they become raving fans and refer you out for future business.

PRO-TIP

Use the Direct Sales Done Right Book and Workbook to increase your conversion!

Engage with current clients. In this section, you are setting aside time each day to engage with your current clients inside of your VIP group, private pages, or community platforms.

Answer emails and messages. This task is simply reminding you to check your inbox and messages on social platforms for customer questions. Timely and individualized customer service does create trust and either allows people to move into raving fans for future referrals or, if you are in direct sales, sets the customer up to become a distributor. Excellent customer service builds trust, creates loyalty, and increases the likelihood of bringing those satisfied customers on as distributors to your team.

Lastly, we have **business and personal development**. We added this to the tracker because, if we don't understand the business we run and continually educate ourselves in the products and services our company offers, we won't be confident in sharing them online.

Educating ourselves about the business we own and how to do our jobs to the fullest potential has been essential to our exponential growth.

Personal development has also been a key area that we know has massively contributed to our business growth. As entrepreneurs, we know that without constant mindset and leadership development we would not be able to scale the way that we have.

We encourage you to listen to audio books, podcasts, and read personal development books that empower you and teach you the skills needed to become the business owner you want to grow into.

See the free resources at *chicinfluencer.com/free-resources* for a list of our favorite personal development books, audios and podcasts.

MY INCOME PRODUCING ACTIVITY TRACKER SAMPLE

Jan. 21, 2024
WEEK OF

			Mon	Tues	Weds	Thur	Fri	Sat	Sun
INCOME PRODUCING ACTIVITIES	**COMMUNITY**	Add Followers	12	20	10	2	15	5	0
		Intentional Connection	5	8	3	5	7	2	0
		Social Media Content (B.E.S. Strategy)	1	1	1	1	1	1	1
		7-10 Stories	✓	✓	✓	✓	✓	✓	✓
		Highlight People: Testimonials/ Shout Outs	✓		✓		✓		
	CONVERSION	DM people who viewed, liked, commented, or followed	✓	✓	✓	✓	✓	✓	✓
		Direct invite to service, experience, or product	20	10	12	17	18	21	0
		Follow-Ups	4	3	6	2	1	28	0
		Direct Invite to Business Opportunity	2	6	0	4	1	1	3
	CUSTOMER SERVICE	Ask for Referrals	1	1	3	0	4	1	0
		Engage with Current Clients	✓	✓	✓	✓	✓	✓	
		Answer Emails & Messages	✓	✓	✓	✓	✓	✓	
		Business Development	✓	✓	✓	✓	✓	✓	✓
		Personal Development	✓	✓	✓	✓		✓	

Weekly Social Media Plan

This is where it all comes together! You are going to organize your content ideas into day and platform (Facebook, Instagram, and TikTok). Take all your ideas through the weekly reflection and brainstorm and map out your content. Consider your marketing goals as well as your B.E.S. Strategy to create an INTENTIONAL weekly social media plan. Don't worry about making the spread perfect! We've left lots of room for you to create. We've included a few considerations for content as well in the Confetti section of the planner!

Considerations for Content

Big Marketing Ideas to Carry into Content

You have a bottom line, so keep that at the front of your mind when preparing the weekly content! What is the message you are trying to convey to your audience? What products do you want to highlight this week? Knowing that goal, what is the big idea that you want to drive home?

Think about what you are trying to "do" with the content. For example, are you trying to sell a new line of mascara that has launched? Are you getting people into the sneak peek event you're hosting? It's important to convey ONE big marketing idea to your audience at a time to avoid confusion.

Content Ideas

Once you've identified your goals and analyzed the weekly trends, it's time to get messy with new ideas, collaboration opportunities, potential roadblocks, and the FUN part of creating content for social media. We've created plenty of space within the weekly marketing calendar for you to write out your thoughts and get all of those reflections and creative ideas onto paper! This is not the space to worry about "staying inside the lines". It's time to get messy with new ideas and get curious about improving past content! Think ahead about how you can lean into current events, trends, and the season. But don't forget, you are marketing with BOTTOM LINE intention. What is the big marketing idea that you are carrying into content? As long as you know what the marketing goal is for the week, we can keep that in mind as the major focus for the week!

While brainstorming your content for the week, think about the purpose of the content you are creating. Ask yourself:
- What is my marketing goal for the week?
- Are there any current events or trends that I need to take into consideration?
- What do I want to post about?
- Am I consistently delivering a message through the B.E.S. Strategy?
- What universal themes do my audience tend to interact with most?

We encourage you to write in pencil without permanency. Sometimes the plan is going to change, and that's okay! **To help you brainstorm what the perfect piece of content will look like, we've included a Content Checklist:**
- Why are you creating this piece of content?
- Bold Tagline
- Personal Connection/Story
- Call to Think or Call to Act
- Image (eye-catching and matches the story)

Clarifying the purpose of your content

Whether you are directly marketing your products and services or adding value through storytelling, we recommend asking yourself the following questions before you post:
- What is the purpose of this content?
- How will this content benefit my audience?
- Is it helpful?
- Is it hopeful?
- Is it healing?
- Is it aligned to my brand and my messaging?
- Is my content aligned to my marketing goals?
- What do I want my audience to do with this particular piece of content?

- How am I measuring success with this particular piece of content?
- Number of shares & saves?
- Action taken?
- Comments left?
- Conversations started?
- Inventory moved?

Implementing the Weekly Social Media Plan

We use this calendar as our guide for what we will be sharing through the week. We do want to note that this is not a fixed plan. There will be times when you have a better idea that you want to swap out for another piece of content. Make sure you don't stay rigid in your approach and allow yourself the flexibility to tweak the plan as your week progresses.

Let me (Melanie) explain why we feel so passionate about this Weekly Social Media Plan. When you have a plan, you are not working on the defense; you are working on the offense of your business. You are able to create content that is driving towards your business and social goals. You are even able to plan ahead with taking the photos for the post you want to make ahead of time. The Weekly Social Media Plan has been a game changer for Chic Influencer, and we are so excited for you to dive in and get started!

You can see in the provided examples on pages 62-63 that I knew my outcome: to sell 20 winter skincare bundles. I knew I had to serve first before I asked for a decision, and adding value is the best way to do that. You are not oversharing; you are not overdelivering; you are creating a trusting community where people will refer you to others because they know you are the real deal!

One last note: This is supposed to be a work in progress! Blank spaces may happen from week to week. We encourage you to sit down weekly and review your analytics and your content. That way you are serving your audience exactly what they want to receive from you BEFORE planning your content

Weekly Social Media Content Ideas

Let's say that on Monday we do a live video on IG to talk about why we're passionate about our business and who we love to serve the most. We talk about our story, connect to our audience, and keep it under five minutes. We will turn that video into an Instagram video with a CTA (call to action). One thing we always ask ourselves is, "What do we want people to do with this content we've created?

Then we refurbish the content:
- We take the video and put it on our FB page with a CTA.
- We take that video and share it through an email to our list of potential customers with a story about us!
- We take the bullet points and make an IG story directing them to the video.

See?! We just created one video and found three different ways to share one idea. HOLY TIME SAVER, right?!

It typically takes about 10-14 days to drive home a particular concept before the audience starts to "lean in", ask questions, and pursue services. We STRONGLY encourage you NOT to get discouraged if you don't see immediate results. If you are committed and willing to make adjustments as you go, this strategy is highly effective. We don't get mad when something isn't working in our favor; we get curious about how we can do better.

When it comes to creating content, make sure your content is not always HARD CALLS TO SELL. People tune out product pushers. Add value in your content; serve, don't sell! If you follow the B.E.S. Strategy, you never have to worry about being too salesly.

Proactive, Not Reactive!
Let's be honest for a moment. There will be weeks that you won't have a lot of time to do your planning. There will be weeks when the creative ideas are not flowing as easily as you would like. There will be times when you are in a crunch for time. That is ok! What is NOT OK is for you to push your social media planner aside and NOT have a game plan. Every time I fail to plan, I am planning to fail!!

PRO-TIP

The secret to *Direct Sales Done Right* marketing? Add value, add value, add value, add value, ask for a decision!

So what does a proactive business look like?

On weeks where you have to sorta kinda wing it, pull out your planner and do some basic work. *Here are a few of our tips to avoid scrambling for content:*
- Write down your focus for the week and what goals you know you need to drive towards.
- Jot down your taglines and some post ideas. Set some realistic social media goals for the week and definitely reflect on what is and isn't working for your social media at this time.
- Be intentional! Even if you feel like you are winging it, you always want to ask yourself, "What is my marketing goal and does this content align to my marketing goal?"
- Try to steer clear of JUST GOING THROUGH THE MOTIONS and documenting your day or checking off the social media boxes. Ask yourself, "Am I posting just to throw up a post? What is the purpose of the content that I am about to share?"
- When in doubt, pull up your old content. (Simply click insights on the homepage of your Instagram account.) Is there old content you can refurbish? Perhaps create a reel from a static piece of content or change up the image and keep the caption!

Still stuck? No worries! In the Confetti section, we'll give you tons of content tips so you're never left to wonder, "What should I post?"

WEEKLY SOCIAL MEDIA PLAN SAMPLE

THINGS TO CONSIDER
- Captions/Hook
- Content I Like
- Hashtags
- Objections
- Collaborations
- Pain Points
- Well Received Content to Refurbish
- Call To Action (CTA)
- Call To Think (CTT)
- Quotables
- Community Driven Content
- Upcoming Events

TYPES OF CONTENT
- Reel
- Carousel
- Video
- Static Post

CONTENT CREATION CHECKLIST
- [ ] Why are you creating this piece of content?
- [ ] Hook
- [ ] Personal connection/story
- [ ] Call to Action (CTA)
- [ ] Image/video (eye-catching and matches the story)

	MONDAY (FB/IG/TK)	TUESDAY (FB/IG/TK)	WEDNESDAY (FB/IG/TK)
CAPTION IDEA:	4 things that are killing your skin	me walking into january with flawless skin	myth: you can't get rid of wrinkles without botox
CTA:	join my winter proof free group	check out my stories to prevent dry skin	comment below if needles freak you out
AUDIO:	puregallussocial	kateryna.sich	myanichol myth and fact
B.E.S. STRATEGY	B [X] E [ ] S [ ]	B [ ] E [X] S [ ]	B [ ] E [ ] S [X]
FB/IG STORIES — MARKETING FOCUS:	winter proof facebook group	winter proof facebook group	winter proof facebook group
VIP GROUP CONTENT	announce the winter proof skin week is coming; invite friends	announce next week's prizes	share daily content topics for winterize your skin

MY MARKETING FOCUS THIS WEEK:
add 50 people to my winterproof your skin group

THURSDAY	FRIDAY	SATURDAY	SUNDAY
FB/IG/TK	FB/IG/TK	FB/IG/TK	FB/IG/TK
CAPTION IDEA: is it possible to get glowing skin while you age? **CTA:** comment "glow" if you want my personal routine **AUDIO:** shannonmckinstrie, see what'd i tell ya **B.E.S. STRATEGY** B☐ E☐ S☒	**CAPTION IDEA:** how to prevent dry saggy skin naturally **CTA:** comment "hydrate" and I will give you my 4 step guide **AUDIO:** talking to the camera; create my own educational reel **B.E.S. STRATEGY** B☒ E☐ S☐	**CAPTION IDEA:** i refuse to let my age be my excuse! **CTA:** if you're done letting age be your excuse, drop a heart **AUDIO:** before/after **B.E.S. STRATEGY** B☐ E☒ S☐	**CAPTION IDEA:** get ready with me! **CTA:** comment "glow" for my personal skin care routine **AUDIO:** take my breath away! **B.E.S. STRATEGY** B☐ E☐ S☒
FB/IG STORIES	**FB/IG STORIES**	**FB/IG STORIES**	**FB/IG STORIES**
MARKETING FOCUS: winter proof facebook group	**MARKETING FOCUS:** winter proof facebook group	**MARKETING FOCUS:** talk about prodcuts in before/after reel!	**MARKETING FOCUS:** talk about prodcuts in before/after reel!
VIP GROUP CONTENT poll: what's your biggest winter skin problem?	**VIP GROUP CONTENT** countdown to free group	**VIP GROUP CONTENT** weekend warrior skin saving advice	**VIP GROUP CONTENT** reminder group starts tomorrow

End of Month Reflection

The end of month reflection is an important part of your marketing and business strategy. At the end of every month, we take time to pause and reflect on our progress towards our goals. As business owners, we have to ask ourselves what is contributing to our success or what is creating a gap between where we want to be and our current situation.

After reflecting, you make decisions for the next month based on the data you have collected and analyzed from last month. This allows you to make small adjustments each month to keep you on the path of success. The first step is to restate your yearly goals. Write down what your monthly goals for the previous month were. Then, write down your progress so far towards the annual goal.

Next, you want to gut check yourself regarding your vision. Are you reading your vision daily? It's important to read your vision daily so that you never lose sight of what you are working towards.

We also give you space each month to double check that your vision is still aligned to your definition of success. There have been times in our direct sales careers where we have tweaked our vision based on what matters most to us.

When you look back over the last month, identify any challenges that stood in the way of achieving your monthly goals. You also want to write out what helped you achieve your goals. By gaining clarity in both of these areas, you can either create a plan for what you need to stop doing, or what you want to make sure is incorporated into next month's action plan. Lastly, if there are tasks, activities, or areas of focus that you need to adjust for next month, get clear on that now.

Once you have finished your monthly reflection, you are ready to create your game plan for the new month. You have used the data from last month to make smart, educated business decisions!

END OF MONTH REFLECTION SAMPLE

December 2023
LAST MONTH

It's time to reflect on last month's business and marketing goals.

MY PERSONAL DEFINITION OF SUCCESS IS: *Success to me means that I'm achieving my business goals & enjoying quality time with my family*

YEARLY GOALS	MONTHLY GOALS	MONTHLY PROGRESS
1. 10k annual income	1. earn $833.33	1. earned $1200 in December
2. advance to Director by Dec. 2024	2. sign up 4 new reps to my team	2. signed 2/4 reps
3. earn rewards trip in Nov. 2024	3. earn $100 trip dollars	3. earned $90 trip dollars

DID I REVIEW MY VISION DAILY? **Y**/ N

DOES MY VISION STILL ALIGN WITH MY DEFINITION OF SUCCESS? **Y**/ N *(If no, take time to update your vision.)*

Reflect on the past month. What helped or prevented you from reaching your goals?

- I didn't give myself enough time to market my online event which prevented my from having more sales
- I forgot to collect emails which made post event follow up challenging
- I didn't hit my recruitment goal, but I have 10 warm leads who I believe will sign up next month

What do you want to do differently next month? What strategies will I implement again next month?

- next month give myself 7 days pre-event to do a full marketing plan
- add a form to my event so that I have a solid system for follow ups
- I will make sure to do an opportunity event and invite personally the people who haven't signed up yet

next
UP...